Ex back!?

# Ex Back!?

The Secret of Getting Back Together

Leonard Kehling & Gabriela Torres

**Bibliographical Information of the Deutsche Nationalbibliothek**
This publication is listed in the Deutsche Nationalbibliographie of the
Deutsche Nationalbibliothek; detailed bibliographical information
can be accessed under http: //dnb.d-nb.de
© 2020 Kehling, Leonard; Torres, Gabriela
Printing, Production and Layout: BoD – Books on Demand
ISBN: 978-3-7526-5391-5

# Content

# Introduction

Almost all of us have experienced the end of a relationship in our lives. Either our partner left us, or we were the ones who left. Most of us probably experienced both.

If we are the one someone broke up with, a world shatters. Even if we see the end of a relationship coming, we do not want to realise this at first. We feel sadness, pain, helplessness and suddenly even the otherwise rational-minded person is entangled in overwhelming sentimental feelings.

In such a situation we often do not know what to do. We are devastated. We are affected by the feelings that we have for our ex and by the pain associated with the separation. It is often as if with a partner leaving us, a part of us dies and we feel emptiness, frustration and helplessness.

We tend to refuse accepting reality or we beg the ex to come back to us. In such situation people are capable of the most desperate and irrational acts as they try to regain the love that has left. Unfortunately most attempts made in this state of uncontrolled emotions are not successful.

However, a break-up does not have to be final. Think about your circle of friends! Is there not the couple X & Y? Were they not separated once? And did they not come together again? Think of all the celebrities whose break-ups and reunions you can follow every week in the yellow press.

There is the possibility of getting back together. If your partner has left you, he or she does not want to be in a relationship with you at the moment. But if you want to be with him or her, there is the possibility of getting back together. In this book we tell you how getting back together works.

You will learn what you can do and what you should not do. We will take you on a journey, during which you will look at your life and your past relationship in a way you have probably not done this before.

Is such a book necessary?

If your partner just broke up with you, you may have already searched in bookshops and on the Internet for help. What did you notice? There is some serious literature available on the topic of separation. There is, however, little advice on how to reunite with the ex. There is some advice available on the Internet – typically for a lot of money. For even more money you might find magic rituals and the likes that are supposed to bring your ex back, but most certainly never do. You are currently experiencing a crisis. You go through a rough time in your life. Unfortunately, that makes some people receptive to various forms of charlatanism.

With our book, we offer you a comprehensive and compact guide on how getting back together with your ex is possible. We want to help you to find a way out of your current emotional struggles. This book is supposed to be a good companion for the coming weeks and months. And we sincerely hope that when you have finished reading this book, you will be glad that you did.

If you want to get back together with your ex and follow our advice, you may often get emotionally exhausted. You may often think that giving up may be the easiest way out. But if you follow the difficult path of our advice, you may be rewarded in the end.

One thing you have to bear in mind though: there is no guarantee that you will get back together with your ex. You have to realise this. However, you can improve your chances of achieving your goal if you follow certain strategies. These we will explain.

Whether they work in your particular case remains to be seen. The secret of getting back together is based on your calmness, self assurance and attractiveness. This is what we will work on.

Even if you will not get back together with your ex, we hope that from reading this book you will gain strength and confidence that will bring you a lot of success in future love matters and relationships.

How to deal with a break-up effectively? Our book starts with advising you what you should do during the first few days after a break-up and what you should avoid.

Furthermore, we would like to invite you on a journey that we call the retreat. You will find out exactly what it is supposed to mean in the corresponding chapter. You will avoid any contact with your ex for a while. During that time you will intensively reflect on your life and your past relationship.

That phase will be followed by what we call the attack. Here, we will help you to become active in order to win your ex back.

We hope that you enjoy reading and that our book helps you to get through a difficult period of your life, and that you will be content with the result of the journey you are about to take no matter what it will be.

Image: photostock / FreeDigitalPhotos.net

# Immediate measures

There are things you must do immediately after the separation from your partner. They are of great importance. Your behaviour during the first few days after break-up has great significance for the further relationship between you and your ex.

## *Take time for yourself!*

First of all, you must accept that you are currently in an extraordinary emotional situation. Accept your lovesickness and sorrow. Allow yourself time to mourn and to cry. It is perfectly fine. This will give you emotional relief. If you have the opportunity to do this, take a few days off. Spend time with friends and family.

## *Accept your lovesickness!*

However, if you feel extremely bad, if you think of nothing else but your ex, if your consumption of alcohol or drugs has increased rapidly, then you must get professional help. Entrust yourself with a good friend and look for a doctor you can trust – a psychiatrist, a therapist or a coach.

As hard as it sounds, but try to enjoy the positive aspects of life as much as you possibly can. Pamper yourself with wellness, good food or some other pleasant things. Show yourself that you appreciate and love yourself.

## *Write down your thoughts and feelings!*

Write down your thoughts and feelings. Write them in a diary or write letters to your ex. However, do not send any of your letters to him or her at this stage. This is an absolute no-go!

Image: Ambro / FreeDigitalPhotos.net

# The behaviour towards your ex

How should you react to your ex' wish to break up your relationship? Follow below advice even if some items do not feel right to you at the moment:

- Accept the break-up completely.
- Express consent.
- Do not try to get your ex back through emotional overreactions.
- Do not whine!
- Do not beg!
- Do not stalk your ex with constant calls, e-mails, SMS or letters!
- Do not let your ex know how bad you feel and how desperate you are.
- Do not try to convince your ex with arguments to change his or her mind.
- Do not tell your ex how much you love him or her.
- All of these reactions would be completely natural and instinctive, but they are all absolutely counterproductive at present and would only increase the emotional distance between you and your ex. He or she would feel being put under pressure.

### *Do not offer or accept friendship!*

Do not accept if your ex offers you friendship. The phrase "Let's remain friends" is unfortunately not a cliché, but actually a reality. Don't offer friendship yourself either.

### *Do not negotiate your feelings!*

Also, you should not try to enter into a "negotiation" with your ex and accept conditions that were under normal circumstances unacceptable to you. If your ex proposes to you, for example, that you can continue to see each other in the context of an open relationship, you have to refuse if you are only interested in a monogamous relationship.

# The retreat phase

You have given yourself the time to mourn? You did not stalk or pester your ex? Well, even if you made some "mistakes", this is not the end of the world, because eventually the effect of such mistakes will fade away over time. And now it's time to let time pass.

The core of what we call retreat is precisely that you distance yourself from your ex. But you must not tell your ex that you do this. Your disappearance should take place suddenly and unexpectedly.

Image: graur codrin / FreeDigitalPhotos.net

In his book "The Passion Trap: How to Right an Unbalanced Relationship" the American psychotherapist Dean C. Delis explains the phenomenon of a passion paradox that arises in unbalanced partnerships. This phenomenon is latently present in many relationships. Most of us are absolutely aware of it and have already experienced it.

The character George Costanza in the American comedy series "Seinfeld" brings it to the point when he says about the women in his life: "When I like them, they don't like me. When they like me, I don't like them. Why can't I act with the ones I like, the way I do with the ones I don't like?"

The idea behind is that in some relationships one partner (the "one-down") loves more than the other (the "one-up"). The person who loves more is dependent on the other, who is the dominant part of the relationship.

### *Lack of attraction.*

A relationship can, of course, fail for a variety of reasons, but in most cases, it is simply the inadequate attraction of one partner that makes the other partner go. Tragically, the abandoned one can often not explain why he or she was abandoned. Sometimes one makes attempts to escape into excuses ("The partner who left me was simply not able to have a relationship."). This can be true. Often, however, one's own brain instinctively rejects the idea that one could not be attractive enough to the partner who left. This is probably manifested in our genes and ensures our survival, because by ignoring such negative aspect, we are again "fit to proceed with life".

Nevertheless, George Costanza's statement is worth considering. Is it not always the case – and not only in love – that we strive for and want what we do not have? And do not things we have bought or goals that we have achieved lose their fascination as soon as we have obtained the objects in question or as we have achieved the desired goals?

## Pressure leads to further distancing.

There can be many reasons for your separation. However, you must realise that your ex has ended your relationship because he or she did not want to be together with you anymore. If you now make the mistakes mentioned in the previous chapter, you put pressure on your ex. Even though you try to get closer to your ex by doing this, you actually create even more space between the two of you. This will only lead to further retreat by your ex and thus increase the distance between both of you.

## Love cannot be obtained by force.

Understanding this principle is absolutely necessary, because you cannot force anyone to love you or to be with you. If you put a loved one under pressure and look for too much closeness, there is a danger that this person will distance itself from you. You may argue that it should be allowed to show a loved one that he or she is loved. This is quite true, but you should only do this if you are sure that the other person loves you, too. "Showing affection" in the current situation is therefore completely inappropriate.

## Accept the current situation!

As the one being left by a partner, one often thinks: "He/she loves me. He/she does just not know/will remember it/must remember, etc..." All of this is not true, though. Particularly in the first phase of lovesickness, we are literally suffering from a loss of reality. We will dive deeper into the various phases of a lovesickness later on.

Our mind refuses to accept the facts, but you need to accept the current situation as it is. At the moment you do not have the power to change anything.

*Dependency is not attractive.*

Through above mentioned statements we also signal that we are dependent on the ex. Dependency is extremely unattractive, though. If another person shows you that he/she depends on you, will you love her? No. This would actually be quite unpleasant for you, because you would rather be together with an independent person, right?

*Be attractive and independent!*

In order to have a chance to restart a harmonious relationship with your ex or to have any harmonious love relationship, the following has to be the case:

1. You must be an attractive and independent partner.
2. Your ex must be interested in a relationship with you again.

We will turn to the second item in the chapter "attack". It is important that the first item is being tackled first.

And something else is important: if you are successful with achieving both conditions, this would lead to a completely new relationship which has only the two protagonists in common with your past relationship. Your goal can only be a life without your ex or a completely new relationship with your ex.

*Love is relative.*

What should give you hope is the following: Delis notes that love is relative. Love can therefore be created. In fact, there are people who cannot save themselves from potential partners, because they either consciously or unconsciously pull love triggers, so that others find them irresistible.

### *You are the "special one"!*

Surely a person who you find completely unsympathetic will not be able to make you fall in love with him/her. However, your ex fell in love with you before. A latent attraction is therefore present, so you do have something that your ex appreciates and likes about you. That means there is a good chance that he/she can fall in love with you a second time.

As mentioned, you have to distance yourself from your ex. This is important in order to disconnect yourself and your ex from the past relationship.

### *Retreat unannounced!*

The important thing is that you disappear quietly and unannounced. Do not tell your ex what you are up to! Just do not contact him/her anymore! The retreat must come absolutely unexpected for your ex. You need to stop any contact with him or her for at least one to two months.

Should your ex contact you during that time, you do not need to hide. Be kind, but restrict any conversation purely to small talk! Keep interactions short and finish them quickly.

This is particularly important in situations where you cannot avoid contact with your ex, e.g. if you still live together, if you have children, or if you see each other at work. Make sure that any communication is restricted to an absolute minimum: advise the details of your move-out, clarify what needs to be clarified concerning your children, discuss only work related things at work, etc.

### *Give your ex the opportunity to miss you!*

You may argue that you do not want to distance yourself from your ex, or that you are afraid your ex might think you have completely accepted the separation, or that your ex will now fully lose any feelings for you if you are not around. If this is what you think, you are wrong. The retreat is actually a powerful weapon, because:

- Your ex will be wondering why you disappeared all of a sudden,
- Your ex now has the opportunity to miss you.

This creates a strong base for your ex to discover the feelings he or she may still have for you.

It is therefore even likely that your ex will try to contact you during that phase. Keep distance, though! Have small talk, but finish any conversation quickly and determined. This shows your confidence.

After all, a retreat demonstrates your self-awareness and your independence. It signals that you take care of yourself. That is extremely attractive.

In case any birthdays, holidays like Christmas or New Year or anniversaries happen to take place during this period: Do not contact your ex! No calls, no letters, no text messages and no gifts! All of this would be extremely counterproductive.

Now, you have to use the time of your retreat productively to prepare for the subsequent attack.

At first, it is very important that you take care of yourself. An important aspect of this is curing the lovesickness, which is typically associated with a separation from a loved one.

According to Austrian psychologist Gerti Sänger, lovesickness consists of five phases:

1. One feels that something is no longer as it used to be. You reflect the past weeks and suddenly notice subtle hints that something had changed.
2. Suddenly you feel paralyzed. Your knees get weak. You feel tumbling. You do not know what to do.
3. You want to negotiate with your partner the continuation of the relationship. You offer compromises.
4. You admit to yourself that the relationship is over. You do not worry about health or work anymore. You are emotionally at an absolute low point.
5. You accept the separation, but you are still mourning. Feelings can vary substantially from day to day, from hour to hour.

*Lovesickness can last for years.*

There are no general rules as far as the length of the individual phases and the total length of the lovesickness are concerned. They vary a lot from person to person, from situation to situation. Lovesickness can last for many years.

During the first days after the separation took place, it is completely okay to be emotionally down. If the circumstances allow, leave your usual surroundings for a while. Visit friends or relatives. Spend a few days away. Allow yourself some time for mourning. Cry.

### *Do something good to yourself!*

Be kind to yourself, though. Pamper yourself. Do yourself something good. Do not be angry about yourself, if you are just passing time unproductively. That is absolutely fine.

However, do not isolate yourself. Talk to friends or relatives. Do something. Relax. Treat yourself for a wellness weekend with your best friend or something like that.

### *Let go!*

Mentally, let go of your past relationship. Here for example, the book "The Language of Letting Go: Daily Meditations on Codependency" by Melody Beattie offers help. Actually written for addiction victims, it offers a daily suggestion on how to deal with the subject of "letting go". The texts provide support and stimulate reflection.

Write a diary. This can also give you support and help to find orientation. Write down your feelings. Write letters to your ex. Do not send them to your ex, though. The letters are to be written exclusively as a means of self-therapy.

### *Think positive!*

Practice positive thinking. Say to yourself: "Everything is good." Repeat these words over and over again. Begin slowly to regain control of your feelings. This is not easy and actually very difficult at first. However, you will see that it works better and better over time.

Once you can think clearly again, start focussing on yourself, your life and your own goals. By doing this, you will gather strength for your upcoming endeavours.

Image: Ambro / FreeDigitalPhotos.net

# Analyse your past relationship

It is important that you reflect on your past relationship. Keep in mind though, that you were probably not very objective when thinking about your relationship in the past. Therefore, try to be as objective as possible now.

*Be as objective as possible!*

Unfortunately, this is not so easy. In the past, you have naturally observed your relationship from your own perspective. Now, try to see it through the eyes of an independent observer. Also, ask a friend for help. Let someone give you an honest third party opinion of your past relationship and compare these views with your own. Outsiders were not emotionally involved in your relationship and can therefore help you to get a clearer picture of the dynamics of your past relationship.

Ask yourself questions about your past relationship. Think about how you behaved with your ex. Were both of you fair to each other?

Repeat the final phase of your relationship mentally and do this as detailed as possible. What did you do and say? What did your ex do and say? Write it all down. Review your records a few times and challenge whether you were truly objective in your assessment.

You can use the following questions as a framework:

- What happened?
- How did I behave?
- Was I fair?
- How did my ex behave?
- What did I feel in the situation?
- Was my ex right?

- What might have happened, had I behaved differently in the situation?

The aim of this exercise is to review the final phase of your relationship as objectively as possible. This will help you to identify possible mistakes on your part.

*To notice your own mistakes is a good thing!*

If you recognize possible mistakes that you made, this is very good. It will help you to behave in a fairer way with your partner in future.

Imagine what might have happened if you had behaved differently in certain situations. Could it be that your ex had then reacted differently towards you? Could it be that the situation had not escalated then?

Of course, this is just speculation. But such exercises are helpful to make us aware of cases in which we did not behave in an appropriate way. Appropriate in the sense of the way we would like to be treated by other people ourselves.

You should also ask yourself the following questions:

- What did I expect from my ex in the relationship?
- What did my ex possibly expect from me in the relationship?
- Could I expect from my ex to meet my expectations?
- Was I too demanding?
- Was I unsatisfied or frustrated with things in my life besides my ex?
- Did I make my ex notice this?
- Did I annoy my ex?
- Did I leave space for my ex?
- Did my ex undermine my ego? If yes, how?
- You may find out that you were disappointed by your ex since he

or she did not meet the expectations that you had for your relationship. This may have been because you both had a different attitude towards your relationship.

If this is the case, you cannot blame your ex for disappointing you. Instead you are the person to blame. You tried to see something in your ex respectively in your relationship with your ex, that if considered objectively was not there. You just saw your ex or your relationship with your ex as you wanted and wished not to notice that this was an illusion.

### *Forget about expectations!*

Often, a relationship does not work out because one partner's expectations towards the other cannot be met. For future relationships, you must therefore free yourself from any expectations that you may have towards your partner's attitude or behaviour.

Jealousy, fear of a break-up, annoying your partner and neglecting the needs of the partner can also play a significant role when a relationship fails.

Considering your previous relationship, ask yourself:

- Was I jealous?
- Did I let this feel my ex?
- Was I afraid of break-up?
- Did I annoy my ex?
- Did I neglect my ex' needs?

Even if it is not possible to generalise, it is often rather men who tend to neglect their relationship and their partner.

Women are more likely to suffer from jealousy and fear of break-up. They are therefore more likely to hang on to a partner or a relationship than men.

Furthermore, you should analyse the personality of your ex to the extent that is possible.

- Did you feel exploited by your ex – mentally, financially?
- Did your ex beat you up or abuse you physically?
- Do you believe your ex is a narcissist?

Prepare lists for each topic. These will help you to analyse your past relationship and will serve you for further guidance. You will read more about this in the next chapter.

## Your lists might look like this:

*List 1) What went wrong in my relationship?*

- .........................................................................
- .........................................................................
- .........................................................................
- .........................................................................
- .........................................................................
- .........................................................................
- .........................................................................
- .........................................................................
- .........................................................................
- .........................................................................

*List 2) How did I behave in the relationship?*

- .........................................................................
- .........................................................................
- .........................................................................
- .........................................................................
- .........................................................................
- .........................................................................
- .........................................................................
- .........................................................................
- .........................................................................
- .........................................................................

*List 3) How did my ex behave in the relationship?*

-   ........................................................................
-   ........................................................................
-   ........................................................................
-   ........................................................................
-   ........................................................................
-   ........................................................................
-   ........................................................................
-   ........................................................................
-   ........................................................................
-   ........................................................................

*List 4) Had it been possible for me to behave differently?*

-   ........................................................................
-   ........................................................................
-   ........................................................................
-   ........................................................................
-   ........................................................................
-   ........................................................................
-   ........................................................................
-   ........................................................................
-   ........................................................................
-   ........................................................................

*List 5) What is my ex' personality?*

- ............................................................................................
- ............................................................................................
- ............................................................................................
- ............................................................................................
- ............................................................................................
- ............................................................................................
- ............................................................................................
- ............................................................................................
- ............................................................................................
- ............................................................................................

Image: Ambro / FreeDigitalPhotos.net

# Know what you want to achieve in life

Now think about you and how your future life should look like. This is easier said than done, and it will most likely require a lot of thought and imagination from you.

Draft a picture of your future life, as detailed as possible and without your ex being part of it. The latter may sound difficult for you at the moment, but it is particularly important. You want to be aware of what you want to achieve in your life, what you want to experience – on your own and irrespective of your ex.

You should also involve the topic of partnership and family in your overall life planning. However, you should not have a concrete future partner like for instance your ex in mind. Rather let your future partner be an unidentifiable person of your imagination.

A good starting point for this exercise is to think about what has happened in your life until now. Take your time for this exercise. Do this when you have a quiet moment on your own. Seat yourself comfortably. Make yourself a cup of tea or coffee. Then when you are in a relaxed mood, think about all the things that happened in your life so far – from your childhood until now. Pick up a pen and a piece of paper and write everything down.

Think about all the things that went well in your life. Also consider negative aspects. Do not judge events. Just write down what happened.

Have you been happy in your life so far? Remember the moments when you felt happy. What were the circumstances at these moments in your life?

Spend a lot of time on these thoughts. Best is to spend several days in a row. Perhaps one or two hours after work every day, once you have come home and made yourself comfortable.

You will notice that after a few days you will have a very comprehensive picture of yourself and of your life. Perhaps you have never thought about your life in this way.

Once you have finished, there are two things to do. First, you filter out all success stories. Make a list of all the positive things you achieved or experienced. Those can be good grades at school, well passed exams, financial success, success in love affairs, success at sport events or anything else you consider important to you. Write down everything that you are proud of having achieved. All the moments which have provided you with the feeling of success in your life so far.

*List of your personal success stories:*

- ..................................................................
- ..................................................................
- ..................................................................
- ..................................................................
- ..................................................................
- ..................................................................
- ..................................................................
- ..................................................................
- ..................................................................
- ..................................................................
- ..................................................................
- ..................................................................
- ..................................................................
- ..................................................................
- ..................................................................
- ..................................................................
- ..................................................................
- ..................................................................
- ..................................................................
- ..................................................................
- ..................................................................
- ..................................................................

You will refer to this list from now on whenever you feel that you need to strengthen your confidence. This is the list that shows you exactly what you can do, what you have mastered and how well you did in different areas. By simply looking at this list and reflecting on your past success, you will boost your confidence and optimism. Try it out! It works.

Furthermore, think about how you can use your achievements in life as a base for your future aspirations.

Actively "brainstorm" with yourself for a few days. Think about your (possible) goals in life. Question them in different ways.

Ask yourself questions like "Who am I?", "What do I want?", "What's my purpose in life or in the world?"

Ask yourself what happiness means to you. Write down how an ideal life looks like to you.

Consider all aspects of your life that come to your mind (health, work, finance, love, hobbies, interests). You may need some days for this exercise. You may also reject some of your initial ideas and revise them after a few days or weeks. This is alright. The most important thing is that you visualise your future life and that the vision you create of it is a positive one.

**Write down your findings in lists like these:**

*List 1) My health:*

- ..................................................................
- ..................................................................
- ..................................................................
- ..................................................................
- ..................................................................
- ..................................................................
- ..................................................................
- ..................................................................
- ..................................................................
- ..................................................................

*List 2) My professional life:*

- ..................................................................
- ..................................................................
- ..................................................................
- ..................................................................
- ..................................................................
- ..................................................................
- ..................................................................
- ..................................................................
- ..................................................................
- ..................................................................

*List 3) My financial situation:*

- .........................................................................
- .........................................................................
- .........................................................................
- .........................................................................
- .........................................................................
- .........................................................................
- .........................................................................
- .........................................................................
- .........................................................................
- .........................................................................

*List 4) My ideal partnership:*

- .........................................................................
- .........................................................................
- .........................................................................
- .........................................................................
- .........................................................................
- .........................................................................
- .........................................................................
- .........................................................................
- .........................................................................
- .........................................................................

*List 5) My hobbies and interests:*

- ..........................................................................
- ..........................................................................
- ..........................................................................
- ..........................................................................
- ..........................................................................
- ..........................................................................
- ..........................................................................
- ..........................................................................
- ..........................................................................
- ..........................................................................

From now on, review your plan for life on a regular basis. At the beginning perhaps once a day, later once a week or once a month. It is
important that you have a clear vision of your future in mind and that
you constantly remind yourself about it in order to keep you focussed
on what matters to you. You can make changes to your plans at any
time.

Image: photostock / FreeDigitalPhotos.net

# Ex back? (Part 1)

Have a look at your notes again after putting them away for a few days. During those days your brain can process your ideas. When you review your notes, you may notice something regarding your ex.

Based on the analysis of your previous relationship, you may find for example, that your ex actually has a narcissistic personality and that he or she abused you physically or mentally. If you compare your previous relationship with the vision for your life, you might notice that your ex would actually not fit into the concept of the ideal future as you have it in mind.

It is also possible that you do not recognise this while reading this book or your notes for the first time, as the separation from your ex took place just a short time ago. However, if you read your notes after some time, you may find that there are actually very good reasons for not being together with your ex anymore.

If you notice this, be glad! This will help you to eliminate your ex from your thoughts and to choose a new path in life. You may also notice how well you feel all of a sudden, now that your ex does not stop you anymore from living the life that you actually want to live. A decision to no longer mourn and to forget about your ex and the past relationship and to start new endeavours instead is very healthy. If you can do this, then you have been "cured"!

However, if you are still convinced that you want to be back together with your ex, and if you are willing to do anything to reach this goal, then there is a difficult path in front of you. At the end of that path, there can be a new relationship with your ex. But there is no guarantee for it. You must keep this in mind.

*There is no guarantee for getting back together.*

It may seem odd, but the less important getting back together with your ex is to you, the more likely it is that your attempt will be successful. You can be proud of yourself if you have a strong personality that conveys this message without saying it: "You! I am the most attractive partner you can possibly get and I give you another chance. If you do not use it, that's too bad for you".

If this is what your ex can sense, chances are good that you succeed. But the path of getting there is cumbersome and requires a lot of efforts. You should expect setbacks, and you must always remember that there is no guarantee for another relationship with your ex.

Think about whether you really want to take on the task of "getting back together with your ex" or whether you want to put your energy rather into alternative future projects.

Do you really want to get back together with your ex?

If so, read on and get ready for a strenuous program.

Image: Louisa Stokes / FreeDigitalPhotos.net

# Becoming attractive

One thing is for sure: Your ex will only be interested in a relationship with you if he or she is attracted to you. You have a great advantage though. Your ex had already fallen in love with you in the past. This means that you definitely have the potential to be the kind of person that your ex is interested in. Your attractiveness may have just faded away during the duration of your relationship.

*You are the kind of person your ex likes!*

At least you know that you can be quite appealing to your ex. What do you have to do now, so that your ex will find you completely interesting again and possibly fall in love with you a second time?

First, consider what is not interesting to your ex. Often after a break-up, the one who is left by his or her partner asks the other one to come back to her or him. Often this goes hand in hand with horrible scenes, crying, begging, etc.

Think! If you are NOT interested in a relationship with someone (and your ex is not interested in a relationship with you in the moment he or she breaks up with you), will this person be more interesting to you when he or she begs you to come back? Of course not. You may find the situation embarrassing, you may want to escape, but clearly you do not want to be in a relationship with that person again.

This is why the complete retreat from your ex is so important! Never stalk your ex! Never beg him or her to come back to you!

You must be an independent, attractive and confident partner! This is the key to your ex being interested in a relationship with you again.

*Increase self-esteem and self-respect!*

But how do you become an attractive and independent object of desire for your ex? Quite simply the same way you would become an attractive object of desire for any other partner.

You should create a program for yourself to enhance your attractiveness. This program should consist of physical and mental components. Your objective is to increase your self-esteem and your confidence. This in turn makes you attractive and independent – for others and ideally also for your ex.

Your program should look like this:

1. Sports

Physical activity is absolutely important. A separation from a loved partner leads to pain and grief. In such a situation your body suffers. Unfortunately people often do not care as much as they should about their body under such circumstances. Through sports you can reduce stress. Stress that was caused by the separation from your ex, but also stress caused by other aspects of our life, for example by your work. You need to take responsibility for the physical condition of our body and improving your health by doing more sports is the best way to get this started.

*Take full responsibility for the condition of your body!*

Do you already exercise regularly? If you do, that's very good! If you don't, you should quickly get used to it. Your ideal sports program includes either 30 minutes of daily cardio training (running, cycling, swimming) or a combined cardio and weight training with at least three exercise days per week. Become member of a local gym and get a personal coach in order to tailor a program according to your needs!

## 2. Wellness, Beauty & Clothing

If you are a woman, this probably does not need to be mentioned separately. You may already be an expert on this. However, even if you are a man, you can get a manicure done or you could consult a hair stylist for advice. If someone gives you guidance on how to look better and you agree with that person, it will boost your confidence. Avoid changing too much though. Remain authentic, but think about your appearance. Also think about what your ex thought about your previous appearance. Did he or she praise you for your great taste, or did he or she sometimes complain about the one or the other thing?

Do not become a completely different person and do not change something about you that you do not want to change, but make sure that you are in general being positively received by the opposite sex.

Often it helps if you have a conversation with a good male friend in case you are a woman or with a good female friend in case you are a man about your current looks. Get advice and go shopping with your friend. If you are in doubt about certain recommendations, simply check with one or two other people.

## 3. Diet

If you are healthy, it makes you look attractive. For this reason, doing sports is so important to you. Physical activity is an essential part of a healthy lifestyle. In parallel to your physical exercises, you should also consider your diet and, if necessary, change it. A healthy diet in connection with doing sports supports health and well being.

Have pleasure in healthy nutrition! There is a countless number of books and internet sites that give nutritional advice and guidance on diets. We do not want to promote any particular form of diet. It is important that you discover the fun and pleasure of living healthy, that any goals you set for yourself are realistic (e.g. when losing weight, if you are overweight), and that you also allow small sins from time to time.

We recommend the following general guidelines: Sugar, milk from cows, ready-made meals, fast food, alcohol and tobacco products are poison for your body. You should avoid these if possible. Every now and then, one or two glasses of wine or beer are perfectly alright though. Consume only occasionally meat. It is best to eat organic meat or venison. This contains less medicine like antibiotics and other pollutants. Wild animals have a more natural way of life compared to industrially bred animals. That has a positive effect on the quality of the meat. Eat fish instead of meat now and then. It is best to eat deep-sea fish or fish from controlled (mountain) lakes, as they are also of better quality. Eat mainly fruits and vegetables (best organic), dairy products such as yoghurt, curd, cheese and nuts. Drink pure water, unsweetened herbal tea and fruit juices. Avoid coffee, alcohol and soft drinks.

Image: photostock / FreeDigitalPhotos.net

# The psychologic component: The power of thoughts

Another important aspect that you should consider on your path to gaining more confidence and more attractiveness is to pay more attention to your thoughts.

You probably think a lot about your ex. Of course you do! Otherwise you would not be reading this book. Your thoughts about your ex may be a constant companion. And they may put a strain on you.

*Use your thoughts to your advantage!*

It is important that you focus and that you use your thoughts to your advantage. For doing this, there are some basic exercises that you can apply:

1. Autogenic training
Autogenic training is certainly a classic among concentration exercises. The goal is to find your inner calm through concentrated breathing and thought exercises. This should eventually lead to mental strength.

In short, autogenic training means that you aim to find moments of rest one to three times a day (if possible in the morning, at noon and in the evening), during which you lie down with your eyes closed and practice a particular chain of thoughts and emotions. At first, this may feel unusual and somewhat strange. After some time, however, you will recognise success. You will become quieter.

A sequence of thoughts to practice could be for instance something like this:

"Sounds are completely irrelevant.
Thoughts come and go.

I am calm.
I am calm and relaxed.

My arms are heavy.
My legs are heavy.

My right arm is warm.
My left arm is warm.
My legs are warm.

My heart beats calmly and evenly.
My breath is calm and smooth.
It breathes me.

My solar plexus feels warm.
My forehead is pleasantly cool. "

You repeat these sentences several times while you charge your thoughts with emotions. You imagine for example how heavy your legs are when you think "My legs are heavy."

There are many books available on the subject that can help you to master this. Also, you may find courses available that you can join.

## 2. Auto-suggestive mantras

By incorporating thoughts about the goals you would like to achieve at the end of your autogenic training, you can use the mental relaxation of the autogenic training to strengthen your confidence. Your thoughts will be absorbed by your subconscious mind as you feel the relaxation of your body when you say "I am calm". This makes you kind of subconsciously programming your goals.

Thoughts can be:
"I am fine."
"I am healthy."
"I am happy."
"I am beautiful."
"I am strong."
"I am relaxed."
"I am attractive."
"I am feminine / masculine."

You can also think about a whole series of such sentences, memorize them, and think them as a mantra throughout the day.

This is much better than constantly thinking about your ex, which just gives you heartache or makes you feel sad. That is alright from time to time, but if you really want to make progress, you have to start thinking positively and this exercise will help you with absolute certainty. Try it out! It helps.

### *Think positive thoughts!*

You become calmer. You can concentrate better. You avoid negative thoughts. You think about positive things which makes you feel better. And you can do it all by yourself using such simple, auto-suggestive techniques.

3. Yoga

Yoga is also highly recommended. However, an appropriate introduction within the scope of this book is not possible as this would go too far. It is best to visit a trial lecture of a yoga class in order to get a first impression. Yoga combines meditative elements and breathing exercises with physical exercises.

4. Meditation

Autogenic training and yoga are forms of meditation. Meditation is a concentration exercise in which the mind soothes and relaxes.

Pure meditation is often understood as an exercise similar to the following example:

- You sit cross-legged with your eyes closed. Your hands touch your knees with your palms pointing to your face.
- You breathe in and out and you pay attention to how you do this.
- You stop all thinking. As this is not so easy, you can help yourself by thinking a completely meaningless mantra. For example, you can think the word "so" while inhaling and the sound "hm" when exhaling. If you have problems with stopping to see mental images, you can imagine these sounds at the same time as written words. "So" and "hm" then kind of override any other thoughts and images that come to your mind.

At the beginning, try this for ten or fifteen minutes. Then extend your meditative state to twenty, thirty and forty minutes.

Schedule some time for such meditative exercises in your daily routine. After a little while you will find that you become more and more calm from doing this.

Image: Ambro / FreeDigitalPhotos.net

# Amusing & Flirting

You may wonder what amusing and flirting have to do with getting back together with your ex. The idea behind it is that you surround yourself with other people who have nothing to do with your ex. In particular, you should be surrounded by people of the opposite sex. Flirt and get to know new people. Go out and have fun! This gives you confidence.

### Meet new people!

Sign up for an online dating service or go to single parties. Flirt with people. Avoid, however, telling people who you date about your ex. And don't overdo it. If you are serious about wanting to get back together with your ex, do not just go to bed with as many new acquaintances as possible. Obviously there are no rules. A mixture of actively looking for attractive partners and some sort of restraint may be the best tactic.

Perhaps you are lucky enough to get to know someone who not only distracts you from your ex, but who is a person with whom you fall in love with. Your ex is not the only person in the world. There are a lot of other people that you could fall in love with.

Some of you will find it difficult to go out and simply enjoy yourself. This is particularly the case when you belong to the above-mentioned category of the "one-down" partners according to Delis' definition.

If you feel that this applies to you, here are a few suggestions.

### *Spend time with people who love you!*

Be good to yourself. This is extremely important. Spend time with friends and family, so that you are surrounded by people who love and like you.

Make sure, however, that you accept reality.

If you panic, remember to think clearly and realistically. Even if it feels like, the end of a relationship is not a disaster. You live. You are healthy. Your life will go on and you will find a way to continue your life – with or without your ex. The pain is finite.

Use the above mentioned methods to find your inner peace and calm, strength and self-esteem.

If you tend to overreact, use the above methods to control your behaviour and your thoughts will become clearer.

Be aware of the submissive "one-down" behaviours you showed in your past relationship. If you are aware of them, it is easy for you to avoid them in future.

### *Have new, brave thoughts!*

It is important that you immediately stop thoughts about submissive behaviour and that you adapt to new, brave thoughts. Once you notice that your thoughts wander into submissive behavioural patterns, consciously change your thoughts instantly.

## *Be angry!*

Also discover your anger. Be angry about the fact that you were submissive. Anger has a very creative potential. Use this to discover your own personal strengths and individuality. Develop self-respect and confidence through being angry.

Think about your future. Do not waste your feelings. Have your own opinion. Never communicate with a complaining tone. Avoid blaming.

If you were in the one-down position in your past relationship, your ex will probably feel an emotional emptiness after the separation, since the one-down is missing as emotional support.

The one-down is no longer subject to the emotional control of the one-up, which strengthens the attractiveness of the former.

If your ex has not yet found a new, better relationship since the break-up, he or she may notice a reduction of his or her self-esteem, which in turn leads to a lack of confidence and to need and uncertainty. The former one-up yearns for the proximity of the former one-down. The ambivalence is gone.

Nevertheless, you should be cautious should a reunion with your ex take place. The new infatuation may not last long and the one-up may never lose the feeling of not living with the really great love that he or she was looking for. However, you can develop strategies for such case once time has come. There is still a long way to go though.

Image: photostock / FreeDigitalPhotos.net

# Ex back? (Part 2)

If you accept and follow the advice mentioned in this book and integrate it into your everyday life, your day-to-day routine should now include the following tasks:

- Focus on personal goals (private–except ex related, professional, financial)
- Healthy nutrition
- Time for sports
- Time for mental exercises
- Time for flirting and establishing new contacts

Schedule these tasks for each day in advance at specific times. This gives you support and orientation. But do not be too strict on meeting all of them each day at the scheduled time.

***Stay at least four to eight weeks away from your ex!***

What you still cannot do is contacting your ex. You should not do this for at least four to eight weeks.

During this time, your focus is supposed to be entirely on yourself. And if you follow the advice in this book, time will pass by very, very quickly.

Whenever you think about your ex, divert your attention immediately to something else, e.g. to the next task of your daily program.

***Reflect!***

However, from time to time, have a look at your notes about your failed relationship. Reflect your past relationship and ask yourself now and then whether this relationship was really worth being continued.

Think of your ex. Shall he or she really be the partner with whom you want to be back together, or are you in doubt? Have you perhaps met someone else in the meantime who is interested in you?

### *If you do not know what to do: Do not do anything!*

If you are not sure what you should do in a relationship, just do nothing. Wait, reflect from time to time, but do not make any – possibly hasty – decisions. You might regret them later on. If you are not convinced that you have the absolutely right idea, think about it for a while or postpone a decision.

### *Keep going!*

If, however, you are still convinced that your ex is the one with whom you should be and want to be together again, then carry on! Be brave! Follow your personal attractiveness enhancement program and firmly believe that you will be back together with your ex.

Faith moves mountains. In fact, if you firmly believe in being back together with your ex, you are so conditioned that your approach is supported by your subconscious mind through instinctive, supporting actions.

Do not allow anybody to bring you off track. However, please keep your sense of reality. Your relationship with your ex is over. What you can possibly achieve is a completely new relationship with your ex, but by no means a continuation of your past relationship. How things could lead to such new relationship can be read in the next chapter.

# The attack phase

## Love & Relationships

There is hardly a subject that has kept people more busy in literature, music and other arts, as well as in everyday life, than love. Whether in books, films or TV series: it's always about love.

Love is something wonderful. But love can also be heartbreaking, agonising and, above all, very complicated. Particularly when your partner leaves you.

But what is love? Most people associate with love to be strongly attracted to another person and thereby to feel happiness.

However, love does not just make you happy. It can also make you very unhappy. Especially if the beloved man or woman does not return love.

Biologists explain love with chemical reactions and hormones, which are supposed to put people in a mental state that leads to them mating for reproduction. In fact, biological aspects such as hormones are very important because they are responsible for the "smell of love", an elementary building block of a love affair.

The term "relationship" derives from the verb "relate". People who begin a relationship with each other relate to each other. Narcissistic people and egomaniacs relate only to themselves. If you want to live in a healthy, happy relationship, you should stay away from such people.

As mentioned in the previous chapter, the foundations of a harmonious relationship lie in the fact that there is mutual attraction between two partners. Usually independent and confident people attract others. You should become this type of person to be attractive again to your ex.

Image: imagerymajestic / FreeDigitalPhotos.net

# The foundations of a harmonious relationship

In order to be able to have a harmonious relationship, you should first of all be a happy partner to yourself. You must love yourself and be happy with you. This makes you loveable for others.

*Love yourself!*

When you enter a relationship with another person, you need to be free from expectations. This will avoid disappointments if your partner turns out to be different from what you had imagined him or her to be in the initial phase of your relationship.

*Do not have too high expectations!*

Treat your partner with respect and be loyal to him or her. Do not show jealousy and do not show that you are afraid of losing him or her. Allow your partner freedom. However, value your relationship and act accordingly.

*Be loyal and respectful!*

Getting jealousy under control is difficult to manage for many people and often leads to conflicts in relationships. Everyone is a bit jealous now and then. After all, jealousy is a sign that one cares for and loves another person. Jealousy has destroyed many relationships though, because if one person is very jealous it tends to annoy the other, pushing him or her away from the jealous one.

*Look out for feedback from your partner!*

Relationship advisers often suggest that people should talk more with each other. Apparently, lack of communication is a problem in many relationships. Always pay attention to how your partner behaves – particularly towards your behaviour and opinions. This is the best way of getting feedback on whether your partner is satisfied in your relationship, or if problems may be on the way. Always pay attention and try to read between the lines. Do not overdo it though and be aware that there is always room for misinterpretation.

Do also not constantly confront your partner with your interpretations. Too much communication may annoy him or her.

Make sure you do not waste your feelings. If you show your partner that you love him or her to an extent that is more than what you receive from your partner in turn, you may become unattractive to him or her. Also, do not make exaggerated and premature gifts.

### Never exert pressure!

Never force your partner into anything. Would you like to move in with him or her? Would you like to have children? Be cautious and do not express such wishes at an early stage of a relationship. When the time is right, plan your future together. Do not make decisions on your own. Set mutual goals.

Show that you have your own opinion. If you nod to everything your partner says, although you do not really agree, you are not very interesting. This does not mean that you constantly have to argue with your partner.

Never communicate with a complaining undertone in your voice. Avoid blaming your partner. Always try to see a situation from your partner's point of view. How would you react to certain behaviour?

If you have any wishes, let your partner know. Do not criticize your partner without a specific reason.

## *Keep your relationship interesting!*

Avoid routine in your relationship. Make sure that you plan joint activities and that you share experiences. This includes romantic moments as well as a nice trip, a shared vacation, exciting and interesting activities or the birth of your mutual child. A relationship in which everyone lives just for oneself will not last very long.

Be tender to your partner. Kiss him or her. But here again, do not exaggerate. Do not urge your partner but rather find a healthy balance, respecting your partner's desire for romance.

Many relationship guides recommend to always maintain a certain tension in your relationship. It is often suggested to male readers that the woman in a relationship has the permanent goal of binding the man to herself or even of controlling him. The moment she succeeds, the man becomes uninteresting. The goal of the man should therefore be to make sure that the woman can never be quite certain about his feelings for her.

Surely that sounds pretty drastic. If, however, you think about the relationship dynamics in your own past or in your circle of friends, you may find that there is some truth in this thesis. Thinking about the topic of proximity and distance again, this does make sense. So what to do? Be careful and do not exaggerate in one way or the other. Show your partner that you have feelings for him or her, but do not throw yourself at the other person. If you are too distanced and closed, there is also a risk that the other person will turn away from you. Try to find the right balance.

## The dream partner

There is no secret recipe for the perfect partner. As we fall in love with different people, we fall in love for different reasons. With one person we like that we both have so much in common or that we have similar interests. With another, we may feel attracted because that person is very different from oneself.

Many people like it when they feel that they and their partners complement each other. This is a very subjective consideration, which can be perceived by outsiders quite differently.

### *Create a vision of your ideal partner!*

In the last chapter, we gave you the advice to think about your life planning in general, including your desired partnership. It can also be very helpful to form a picture of the kind of person you would like to be with. By this, of course, we do not mean a picture of your ex, but of an imaginary dream partner. Think about how a person should be like and what kind of attributes he or she should have.

For example, consider the following criteria:

- Age
- Appearance, ethnic background
- Personality, characteristics
- Interests, hobbies
- Religion, political attitude, profession, education
- Marriage / children

Write your preferences down and compare your ideal partner with your ex. Are there matches? Maybe. Probably there are a few, if your break-up was not so long ago. However, go through this "dream partner profile" over and over again. It would not be unusual if you find out that the person who broke up with you is actually quite different from your dream partner. If this is the case, be glad about having found out and forget about your ex! In this case he or she may indeed not have been the right partner for you.

Image: photostock / FreeDigitalPhotos.net

# The attack

Have you successfully implemented your attractiveness enhancement program? Do you live up to it? Have you thoroughly thought about your personal goals? Do you know what you want to achieve in your life – privately, professionally and financially?

Have you been paying attention to your diet? Have you been exercising regularly physically and mentally?

Have you been going out? Did you have fun and did you make new contacts? Have you come across any potential new partner?

We hope that you have had some successful weeks and that your new activities motivated and inspired you, that they strengthened your confidence and made you an even more attractive partner.

If you have found a new (potential) partner in the past weeks, or if you have realised that it is not worth giving another chance to your ex, we can only congratulate you. Forget your ex and enjoy your new life! It is much easier to start from scratch with a new partner.

However, if you are still interested in a new relationship with your ex, this now calls for an attack. You will have to seduce your ex. Be aware that there is no guarantee that your ex will fall in love with you again, but there is a great chance that this might happen.

What to do?

After four to six weeks of absolute silence between you and your ex, you will now get in contact with him or her again. However, there are some things to consider, as you will read below. If your meeting is going well, you will meet again and again, until you are a happy couple again.

Image: nuttakit / FreeDigitalPhotos.net

Now, call your ex. Do not send him or her a letter, a text message, an e-mail or any other kind of written message. The personal contact is absolutely important, as your voice and the way you speak will show your newly gained confidence.

You could also arrange to meet your ex "by chance". However, you should choose this option only if you feel very confident that you are able to handle such direct confrontation. If you are sure about this, arrange for a convenient opportunity to meet casually and seemingly by coincidence (e.g. at work, in your ex' favourite coffee place, etc).

Keep in mind that a first conversation since your break-up does not have to be a positive one. It may well be the case that your mood significantly deteriorates during the conversation. In the case of a telephone call, your ex will at least not notice your facial expressions.

### *Call your ex!*

The purpose of your telephone call is to arrange a meeting. It has to sound like you do not call for an important reason. You just pretend to intend to have a little chat with your ex. All very casual. At least this is what it has to seem like.

You must appear charming, calm and relaxed to your ex. Just the fact that you call your ex like that will make him or her wonder. This is good, because it gives your call a mystical touch. And that in turn makes you interesting.

Call your ex during the week and not at the weekend. If possible, at a time when you are fairly certain that your ex is at home alone – best in the evening.

Before calling, remind yourself that you are an independent, attractive and confident person. You do not need your ex. Whether or not your ex will meet with you is absolutely not important to you. Convince yourself about this. If you are no convinced, do not call yet.

Call your ex in a convenient moment and wait for him or her to answer the phone. If you do not normally call with a suppressed number, do not call this time with your telephone number being suppressed.

If your ex answers the phone, be friendly and ask how he or she is doing. After a few minutes of small talk, simply ask your ex in a casual way to meet with you.

### *Plan for a joint activity in advance!*

For this you should have already considered a suitable option in advance. Best is an ordinary, casual activity rather than something romantic. It should not take longer than half an hour or maximum one hour. The classic flirt option – a cup of coffee in a nice coffee place – is just as suitable as a game of badminton. Think about something that is fun for both of you, but that is at the same time innocent, so that your ex does not suspect that you want to persuade him or her to get back together with you. Clearly, this is not what you want.

Propose for the meeting to take place within a few days (preferably within five to seven days after your phone call). This is necessary so that your ex can develop a certain excitement prior to your upcoming meeting.

Suggest for the meeting to take place on a weekday. On Friday or Saturday evening, you have better things to do. Maybe your ex already planned something for the weekend. This topic is best left untouched.

If your ex does not answer the phone, do not call a second time on the same day. Do not try to reach him or her more than once per day. If you have called on three consecutive days and your ex has not answered the phone during that time or has not called you back, wait at least two weeks before calling again. Everything else would be annoying. Also, do not leave a message on your ex' answering machine.

### *Be patient if you cannot reach your ex!*

If you do get your ex on the phone and it turns out that your ex has no interest in meeting with you, accept this immediately without any further comments. Pretend to remain in a good mood, change the topic of the conversation and say goodbye after a few minutes. Perhaps your ex will still get in touch with you after a few days, because you made such a good impression on him or her, maybe he or she was just too shy or hesitant to immediately agree to meet with you. If you do not hear from your ex, you have to wait at least another six weeks before giving it another try.

In the event that your ex is not sure whether he or she should meet you, tell your ex in a humorous way that there is nothing wrong with the two of you meeting again.

It is only important that you give a good impression during your first phone call after your break-up. You will not be able to attract your ex to you again just by talking over the phone. For this, you will use the upcoming meeting with your ex.

# The first meeting

Now you have managed to arrange the first date with your ex since you broke up. Even if this is not a date in the classical sense, the same rules apply, of course.

However, you must wait with trying to seduce your ex. The purpose of this first meeting is just to create a general understanding between you and your ex on the basis of which further meetings can take place.

*Prepare yourself well for meeting your ex!*

The meeting should take place in a relaxed atmosphere and it should not last longer than thirty to sixty minutes. When there is little time available, the time you spend together is scarce and valuable. When your meeting is short and you have a good time with each other, chances are that your ex longs for a new meeting. If your date lasts too long, there is a risk of boredom coming up or of your talks going too far for the time being.

For each date prepare yourself appropriately:

- Carry on with your attractiveness enhancement program in order to be in an optimal physical and mental state for your meeting.
- Consider in advance what clothes or jewellery you will wear for your date. You should look attractive, but you should not exaggerate.
- Rehearse the meeting with your ex mentally a couple of times in advance. This prepares you like a sportsman for a competition. It will make the meeting seem more like a routine which makes it more relaxed.
- Get yourself into a good mood right before the meeting takes place. You want to appear relaxed, cheerful, happy and optimistic in front of your ex. So this is how you have to be like.

The topics you should talk about at your first meeting should not be too sophisticated, they should be more like extended small-talk. However, you should subtly raise your ex's interest in your person.

### *Show that you are interesting!*

For this purpose, you should carefully mention a couple of events which took place during the weeks since your break-up and which make you look good and interesting to your ex. This could be a funny anecdote of a trip with friends. In particular, stories in which the other sex plays a role subtly point out that you are very likely meeting with people of the opposite sex and that you enjoy yourself with them.

Be careful, however, and do not exaggerate. If you tell your ex about with whom you had sex or about meeting online dates, it may be embarrassing for you and it may turn your ex off. You are an interesting person. That is why your ex was together with you in your first relationship. That interest in you is what needs to rekindle.

In addition, you should allow your goals and future plans to subtly flow into your conversation. Your ex should get the impression that you are independent and that you carry out important and interesting projects in your life.

Your ex may be wondering how you have overcome the break-up so quickly and whether it mattered to you. This is exactly what you want to achieve! This makes you attractive and it makes you appear extremely confident and independent.

### *Do not mention your previous relationship!*

Never talk about your past relationship. What is over, is over. Your goal is a new relationship with your ex. For this you must be attractive to him or her. Everything that has to do with your old relationship is currently counter-productive. If your ex brings up your old relationship, let him or her talk about it, but remain quiet.

### *Listen actively!*

Most important of all, let your ex talk. Whoever talks, releases hormones of happiness. This is particularly true for women. You have not seen each other for a long time. So there may be a lot to talk about. Be an active listener. Think sexy thoughts. For example, think about having sex with your ex. This will positively affect your charisma.

Be prepared for your ex to tell you about his or her new girlfriend or boyfriend. Do not let that have a negative effect on your intentions. When your ex is already in a new relationship, this does not mean anything. A new relationship can be over as quickly as it has begun.

### *Smile!*

Make sure you smile at your meeting, although you should not put an unnatural permanent grin on your face. A relaxed smile, however, makes you seem very sympathetic. Look your ex in the eye. Keep as much eye contact as you can without staring at your ex.

### *Mirror your ex!*

Mirror your ex. Do this, however, subtly, otherwise your ex will think that you imitate him or her. Subtly mimic your ex's body posture, head movements, facial expressions, voice, breathing and movements. Subconsciously this will let you appear sympathetic to your ex.

### *Be sympathetic!*

Use the words "you" and "we" and avoid using "me" and "I". Let your facial expression be lively and show emotions. Say the name of your ex – ideally every five minutes. This creates intimacy, closeness and sympathy. People like hearing their name.

### *Touch your ex!*

If the opportunity comes up, touch your ex seemingly inadvertently. For instance, touch his or her fingers when you intend to reach something, or while walking subtly put your hand on his or her back. It has to be natural and it should not appear deliberate. It is useful if you practice such flirt techniques (active listening, mirroring, smiling, light touching, etc) in advance during your retreat phase with other people on some of your dates. You should do this especially if you are unskilled and if your last dates prior to your relationship with your ex took place some time ago.

### *Do not plan to meet again!*

The most important thing at the end: Do not make any plans for another meeting! If your ex talks about a possible next meeting on his or her own, simply reply that you will contact him or her regarding that matter. Be absolutely non-committal. Your ex does now not know whether he or she will see you again. If both of you were in a good mood at your date and if you had a good time, your ex may now think a lot about you. Perhaps he or she will even contact you on his or her own shortly after your date.

Image: nuttakit / FreeDigitalPhotos.net

If the first meeting with your ex went well and if you feel good about it, carry on like before. Dedicate yourself fully to your attractiveness enhancement program, enjoy yourself and have fun.

Then wait for approximately two weeks and call your ex once again. Arrange for a date and proceed according to the same scheme as the first time.

From now on, continue to follow this pattern:

- Wait for about two weeks after your meeting.
- Call and make a new appointment with your ex.
- Meet your ex.
- And so on...

### *Be in a good mood!*

It is important that you are always in a good mood on your dates, that you always do something different on them, that you do not put any pressure on your ex and that you do not speak of your past relationship.

Now your ex has the chance to see you regularly again. He or she can notice your attractiveness, your confidence and your charm. You can become attractive to your ex once again and he or she can fall in love with you a second time.

After some time and various dates, there may be a romantic moment that opens up the possibility for getting together again and for a new relationship. Do not force this moment. Let your ex be the active one. You have created the best opportunities for you to be successful.

### *Be patient!*

Always remind yourself that the first romantic moments do not necessarily mean that you are now back together. This can take quite some time. So be patient.

Image: Piyaphon / FreeDigitalPhotos.net

That is the theory. As mentioned several times, there is no guarantee that this plan will work. If you stick to it though, you position yourself in the best possible way to be successful.

Alternative methods do hardly exist. To increase your own attractiveness, to enter subtly again into your ex' life and to trigger love mechanisms with this is really the only way to get back together with your ex.

*Be prepared to experience setbacks!*

Keep an optimistic attitude on everything you do, but do not take the whole thing too seriously. Be prepared for setbacks and make it clear to yourself that a life without your ex can be just as wonderful or even greater than spending your life with your ex.

*Have a plan B: a life without your ex!*

If you experience setbacks, e.g. if you become aware that your ex has a new partner, do not let yourself get upset and stay on course.

But do not get involved into something that does not bring you success. If you have been trying to contact your ex for a long period of time without getting any response to your contact requests: Give up! Focus on your own life and follow the plans and goals that you have defined for yourself during the retreat phase.

There are people who try to get back together with their ex for years and years. There are cases where this actually succeeds, but do not count on this to happen.

*Be happy with yourself!*

You will find someone with whom you will be happy. More importantly, you are happy with yourself and without someone else! This is the key to success.

We wish you all the best and great success in all your endeavours!

Image: imagerymajestic / FreeDigitalPhotos.net

# Literature:

Beattie, Melody, *The Language of Letting Go: Daily Meditations on Codependency: Daily Meditations for Codependents*, 1990

Delis, Dean C. / Phillips, Cassandra, *The Passion Trap: How to Right an Unbalanced Relationship: Where Is Your Relationship Going?*, 2002

Sänger, Gerti, *Liebeskummer – Eine Chance*, 2000

# NOTES

# NOTES

.......................................................................

.......................................................................

.......................................................................

.......................................................................

.......................................................................

.......................................................................

.......................................................................

.......................................................................

.......................................................................

.......................................................................

.......................................................................

.......................................................................

.......................................................................

.......................................................................

.......................................................................

.......................................................................

.......................................................................

.......................................................................

.......................................................................

.......................................................................

.......................................................................

.......................................................................

.......................................................................

# NOTES

........................................................................................
........................................................................................
........................................................................................
........................................................................................
........................................................................................
........................................................................................
........................................................................................
........................................................................................
........................................................................................
........................................................................................
........................................................................................
........................................................................................
........................................................................................
........................................................................................
........................................................................................
........................................................................................
........................................................................................
........................................................................................
........................................................................................
........................................................................................
........................................................................................
........................................................................................

# NOTES

# NOTES

# NOTES

# NOTES

..................................................................................................
..................................................................................................
..................................................................................................
..................................................................................................
..................................................................................................
..................................................................................................
..................................................................................................
..................................................................................................
..................................................................................................
..................................................................................................
..................................................................................................
..................................................................................................
..................................................................................................
..................................................................................................
..................................................................................................
..................................................................................................
..................................................................................................
..................................................................................................
..................................................................................................
..................................................................................................
..................................................................................................
..................................................................................................